The Library of
NATIVE AMERICANS

The Ohlone
of California

Jack S. Williams

The Rosen Publishing Group's
PowerKids Press™
New York

For my parents, Jack and Louise Williams

Published in 2003 by The Rosen Publishing Group, Inc.
29 East 21st Street, New York, NY 10010

Photo and Illustration Credits: Cover © Ann Thiermann, courtesy Santa Cruz Museum of Natural History; p. 4 Erica Clendening; p. 7 mural by Ann Thiermann, courtesy Santa Cruz Museum of Natural History; pp. 8, 20, 23, 26, 50 courtesy of the Phoebe Apperson Hearst Museum of Anthropology and the Regents of the University of California (p. 8, 15-18181; p. 20, 15-18185; p. 23, 15-5018; p. 26, 15-14988; p. 50, 15-23203); pp. 10, 24 courtesy of Mission San Rafael Arcangel, photo © Cristina Taccone; p. 12 © Gallo Images/COR-BIS; pp. 15, 32, 34, 49 © Cristina Taccone; p. 17 courtesy of the de Saisset Museum, Santa Clara University, photo © Cristina Taccone; p. 37 collection of Mission San Francisco de Asís, photo by Cristina Taccone; p. 38 courtesy Mission San José, photo © Cristina Taccone; pp. 41, 46 courtesy of The Bancroft Library, University of California, Berkeley; p. 42 courtesy Santa Cruz Mission State Historic Park, photo © Cristina Taccone; p. 52 courtesy Geo-Images Project, Department of Geography, University of California at Berkeley.

Book Design: Erica Clendening

Williams, Jack S.
    The Ohlone of California / Jack S. Williams.
        p. cm. — (The library of Native Americans)
    Summary: Describes the culture, government, arts, and religion of the Ohlone people of the central California coastal region, through over one thousand years of their history.
    Includes bibliographical references and index.
    ISBN 0-8239-6430-2
    1. Ohlone Indians—History—Juvenile literature 2. Ohlone Indians—Social life and customs—Juvenile literature. [1. Ohlone Indians. 2. Indians of North America—California.] I. Title. II. Series.
E99.O32 W56 2002
979.4004'9741—dc21
                                                                          2002003760

There are a variety of terminologies that have been employed when writing about Native Americans. There are sometimes differences between the original language used by a Native American group for certain names or vocabulary and the anglicized or modernized versions of such names or terms. Although this book contains terms that we feel will be most recognizable to our readership, there may also exist synonymous or native words that are preferred by certain speakers.

Contents

The Ohlone and Their Neighbors

NEVADA

Coast
Miwok

San
Francisco ○

Ohlone

Northern
Valley
Yokuts

CALIFORNIA

*Monterey
Bay*

Monterey ○

Esselen

Salinan

Southern
Valley
Yokuts

Pacific
Ocean

One

Introducing the Ohlone

Towering mountains and foggy valleys guard the coastline of central California. Over the centuries, many different people have lived on this land. Today, there are few obvious signs of a Native American presence. However, if someone looks carefully in the right places, there are markers of a nearly forgotten era. Broken bits of stone and huge piles of shells tell of a time when the lands between San Francisco Bay and Monterey Bay were the home of a people we call the ancient Ohlones. They built an amazing culture that allowed them to prosper for more than a thousand years.

The Spanish settlers often called the Native Americans of the area Costaños , or coastal people. This word was later modified into Costanoan. During the last quarter of the twentieth century, many of the descendants of these people decided that they preferred the name "Ohlone." No one is certain from where this word came. It may have been the name of a large village in the San Mateo area. Other experts believe that it is a word used by Native Americans in the east that meant "western people." Although they spoke languages that shared certain important features, the Ohlones did not think of themselves as belonging to any large group. Instead, they identified themselves according to their village communities. When

This map illustrates the homeland of the Ohlone, between San Francisco Bay and Monterey Bay in present-day California.

The Ohlone of California

the Spanish arrived in 1769, the Ohlone nations included the Karkins, the Cochenyo, the Ramaytush, the Tamyen, the Asaswas, the Mutsun, the Rumsen, and the Chalon.

No one is certain when the first Ohlones appeared. Most experts agree that sometime between forty thousand and thirteen thousand years ago, people from Asia came to North America. After traveling from Siberia to Alaska using a frozen land bridge, the immigrants slowly moved south. By twelve thousand years ago, some of the people had reached the tip of South America.

During the thousands of years that followed the arrival of the first people, many different groups moved up and down the coast of California. One society that eventually made its home in the region spoke a language from the Penutian family. Their relatives included many Native Americans who made their homes in the Pacific Northwest. As a result, numerous scholars believe that the Ohlone came from the north.

The Penutian-speaking people may have arrived in peace, or they may have pushed the original inhabitants out of the region. By about 500 CE, the direct ancestors of the Ohlones had probably built their villages near what is now San Francisco and Monterey. Many of the Native Americans who lived to the east of the Ohlones spoke similar languages. However, by the time that European explorers arrived in the region, the Penutian-speaking Native Americans of California had been living in their different homelands for so long that they felt no particular sense of kinship with the other Penutian speakers.

This painting is a modern artist's reconstruction of what an early Ohlone village might have looked like.

The Ohlone of California

Some scholars and Native Americans believe that the Ohlones are descendants of the first nations to live in central California. They believe that the Ohlones have always lived in the areas where they were found in 1769.

When the Spaniards began to colonize central California, they were amazed that the people they found spoke so many languages, and were so fiercely independent from each other. Like many of the other people of the California coast, the Ohlones lived in well-organized villages made up of brush-and-reed houses. There were about five thousand to ten thousand people living in the area in 1770.

The Ohlones and Europeans did not build the kind of relation-ship that either group had wanted. After the end of the sixteenth century, Spanish ships began to visit the region and occasionally

These two baskets were collected from Mission Santa Cruz around 1885. Experts believe they probably represent examples of Ohlone basketry.

traded with the natives for supplies. In 1769, Spain invaded the Ohlone country and began to establish military settlements. Between 1770 and 1846, most of the Ohlones were incorporated into the Spanish Empire, and later the Republic of Mexico. After 1846, the Native Americans desperately hung on to their roots during a century of discrimination and hatred. In the second half of the twentieth century, Ohlones began to reestablish their place as one of the most important native groups in California.

This book provides information about some important parts of the Ohlone story. In the pages that follow, you will get a chance to examine some of the major events that have taken place since Europeans arrived in the Ohlone region in 1602. You will also read about the way that the early Ohlone people lived.

Two
Ohlone Technology

When Spanish settlers came to live in central California in 1769, what was the Ohlone way of life like? What kinds of things did the Ohlone make and use? What kind of houses did they live in? The Ohlones built settlements with unique characteristics. They produced many different objects that were both beautiful and useful. Nearly everything that the Ohlones created were produced using the natural resources that surrounded them.

Living with Nature

The Ohlones felt a close tie to the natural world. Their lands were filled with a fantastic variety of plants and animals. The hills and mountains were covered by a combination of grasslands, redwoods, and oak forests. The coast included large rocky areas as well as vast marshlands that were thickly covered by reeds. Every part of the Ohlone world had rivers, streams, and springs that gushed abundant freshwater.

The natives found abundant sources of food in the plants that surrounded them. From the land, they harvested dozens of plants, grasses, and nuts. Their surroundings also provided many kinds of game. Ohlone men hunted many different kinds of animals, including

The Ohlones used many different kinds of chipped stone objects like those pictured here, including projectile points, drills, and knives.

bobcats, coyotes, ducks, grizzly bears, mice, snakes, and a wide variety of insects. The Ohlone people ate all the different kinds of eggs that they could find. Because of their religious beliefs, the Ohlone did not hunt or eat buzzards, eagles, frogs, owls, or ravens.

Every year, the Ohlones burned the open spaces that surrounded the trees in their community's forests. This action increased the amount of food that the land would produce by making it easier for wild grasses and flowers to grow. These plants produced seeds that served as food for the Native Americans and many of the animals that

they hunted. These controlled burns also helped to prevent more dangerous natural fires by eliminating hazardous brush. Early Spanish settlers described these areas as beautiful grassy meadows without ever realizing that Native Americans had created them.

Plants and animals were also harvested from the Pacific Ocean. The Ohlone hunted sea

Quartz crystals like these were used in Ohlone healing ceremonies.

otters, seals, and sea lions. They also ate many different kinds of shell-fish, fish, and sea plants. When a whale occasionally washed up on the shore, its meat and fat were also eaten.

The Ohlones depended on many different kinds of stones and minerals. Salt, which was collected from along the shorelines, was an important item in everyone's diet. A variety of natural substances, such as carbon, were used to create paint. Other minerals, such as quartz crystals, were used in healing ceremonies. Rocks were essential for the creation of many of the basic tools that were used everyday. Plants and trees were important sources of raw materials. The wood was carved into hundreds of kinds of tools, such as bowls, posts, bows, spears, knife handles, and paddles.

Ohlones' attitudes about using nature were very different from those of Europeans. They believed that natural resources were alive and had to be treated with respect. When they used something, they often said a special prayer. They believed that they had to balance their needs with those of other kinds of life.

Although they often tried to live in harmony with their surroundings, the Ohlones still faced many difficult natural challenges. There was always the danger presented by animals, such as grizzly bears, rattlesnakes, and wolves. Storms, diseases, droughts, and other natural catastrophes took place. The Ohlones' lives were often filled with pleasure, but they also experienced many tragedies and sorrows.

Clothing and Body Decoration

The mild climate of central California made it possible for the Ohlones to live without the use of very much clothing. The men and young children generally went about their lives naked. When it was cold or wet, the Ohlones used robes, short capes, or blankets. Sometimes, the men covered their bodies with mud to protect them from the cold. The soles of everyone's feet were thickened by a lifetime of walking without shoes.

Unlike many other Native Americans, the Ohlone men often wore beards and moustaches. Their hair was usually tied up in the back, near the tops of their heads, or worn in braids. They sometimes wore hairnets. When they went hunting, the Ohlones sometimes wore deer masks and painted their bodies with special symbols designed to help them accomplish their objectives. The women wore more clothing than did the men. Every adult female had a two-piece skirt. Ohlone women also wore tattoos. They decorated their shoulders, chest, chins, and faces with a combination of dots and lines. By using different kinds of plants, it was possible to make the tattoos look black, blue, or green. Every village used symbols that made it easy for other Ohlones to recognize where a woman grew up. Their long hair usually fell over their shoulders. The women sometimes protected their heads with small baskets that were worn as caps. They could often be seen carrying food in baskets that rested on their backs, and that were held in place with a strong headband. Some of these burden baskets held up to 200 pounds (90.7 kg) of cargo.

Both men and women enjoyed wearing jewelry. The items that they used included bracelets, hairpins, pendants, earrings, nose plugs, and strings of beads. During celebrations and rituals, the Ohlones sometimes wore elaborate headgear made from bones,

Baskets played an important role in many different parts of Ohlone life, including food preparation and gathering.

feathers, seashells, and white bird down. They also wore skirts made from bird down, feathers, milkweed, and grass. Other ceremonial items included feather cloaks and robes.

The Ohlones combined clay, charcoal, ashes, grease, and red minerals, called hematite and cinnabar, to create paints that they used to decorate their bodies. The most common colors were black, white, red, and brown. Different designs were worn during ceremonies, warfare, and hunting. Many villages had their own sets of symbols.

Villages

The lives of the Ohlones were spent in villages. There were probably about fifty of these settlements when the Spanish settlers arrived in California in 1769. The villages varied in size. Some included as few as fifty people, while others may have had as many as five hundred inhabitants.

Ohlone settlements were always built close to a supply of flowing water. They were often created at locations that overlooked rivers, streams, springs, or marshes. Sometimes they were built on the top of large piles of shell and ash called middens. Over the centuries, these piles sometimes grew to be an amazing size. Other villages were created on hillsides or hilltops. The houses of the village were laid out around a large, open space.

The Ohlones lived in small huts made out of poles, grass, ferns, bulrushes, or reeds. Each dwelling was occupied by one or two related families. The houses had circular floor plans and ranged from 6 to 20 feet (2–6 m) in diameter. People slept on top of reed mats or blankets next to the walls. When it rained, a piece of animal skin was used to cover the opening. The family dug a hearth, or fire pit, in the center of the room. A hole was left in the middle of the roof. It allowed sunlight into the house and made it possible for smoke from the hearth to escape. The fire was used to heat the house and to cook. Most of the meals were prepared out of doors. The houses also protected the family's other property, such as furs, blankets, pouches, hunting equipment, fishing gear, and baskets.

Most Ohlone settlements also included a single larger home that was reserved for the use of the chief, or community leader. Much of the extra space inside was occupied by baskets filled with food. Sometimes the room was used for special rituals and dances. One

This modern recreation of an Ohlone house is from the de Saisset Museum of Santa Clara University.

early account from 1769 suggests that these buildings could be very large. The Spanish visitors estimated that one such structure could easily hold two hundred people.

Every Ohlone family had one or more granaries. These small structures looked like baskets elevated above the ground on four poles. The granaries were used to store acorns and other seeds that were eaten during the winter.

Even though they had to work hard, the Ohlones still liked to play games. Some of the contests involved two teams, that attempted to score by pushing a large wooden or stone ball across a line. One contest was a lot like the modern game of kickball. On one side of the village, there was usually a large, flat, open area with a smooth surface that was set aside for use during sporting events.

 The Ohlones also set up various kinds of pole-and-thatch coverings for shade. Woven mats were also used to create temporary windbreaks. During the day, men and women often sat in the shelter of these structures while they prepared food or made objects, such as jewelry and tools.

At least some of the villages had oval dance enclosures that were made out of brush. Many of the places where the Ohlones lived and worked were also seen as sacred places. They often planted prayer sticks decorated with feathers at these locations and treated them with special respect.

The northern Ohlones usually burned their dead. In the south, only the bodies of the most important people were burned; everyone

Each village had at least one sweat lodge. These structures were similar to the Ohlone houses except that they were partially buried in the ground. A pole decorated with strips of rabbit skin and feathers marked most sweat lodges. Inside the cramped building a fire produced billowing smoke and intense heat. The interior walls were covered by mud. A hole in the roof allowed the smoke to slowly escape. Sweat lodges were mainly used by men. In order to get in and out of the building, they had to crawl through a low doorway. Inside the sweat lodges, the men used the smoke for cleansing and healing. They also kept their hunting gear and weapons here. There was room for up to about eight people. After they had been inside the structure for a while, the men used curved sticks or deer ribs to scrape away their sweat. Sometimes they sang special songs while they were inside. Many men followed their stays in the sweat lodge with a swim in a nearby creek.

else was buried. The Ohlones usually destroyed all the property of the person who passed away. The ashes or other remains were buried near their villages. Ohlone religion prevented them from talking about the dead, or even mentioning their names.

Although each village had a well-known main location, many of the people often worked in other parts of their territory for extended periods. Each year, the harvesting of wild plants and animals would require the Ohlones to build smaller, less permanent camps and villages. People who were sick or too old to work stayed at the main village site. Eventually, when their tasks had been completed, the working people would return to their main village.

Because their settlements were easy to build, the frequent movement of the communities did not make too much extra work. Unlike other Native Americans, the Ohlones could find everything that they needed within a

This coil gift basket made by the Ohlones is decorated with white glass beads.

relatively short distance. Very few villages included territories greater than 100 square miles (259 sq. km).

Cooking

Ohlone women created meals using many different cooking methods. Some of the wild plants they ate, such as acorns and buckeyes, were ground into powder and soaked in freshwater to remove poisonous substances. Many of the shellfish, such as abalone, had to be tenderized by pounding them with heavy stones before they were cooked. Some things, such as wild berries, could be eaten without any preparation.

The Ohlones cooked many items by roasting them over an open flame. Other foods were steamed or smoked over slow burning fires. Some dishes were prepared in pit ovens. These devices consisted of large holes that were dug into the ground. A fire was built in the pits. Stones were slowly added to the flames. When the rocks were red hot, poles were used to drag the rocks out of the pit. Some of the rocks were put back into the hole, along with food, such as shellfish or meat wrapped in leaves. Additional hot rocks were piled on top. After a few hours, the food was ready.

The Ohlones did not use pottery or stone bowls for cooking. Instead, they prepared stews and similar liquid dishes using tightly woven baskets. Stones that had been heated in a fire were placed into the mixtures. The contents had to be stirred constantly or the stones would burn holes in the baskets.

A similar set of methods was used to roast seeds and nuts. Small pieces of burning wood were tossed onto basket trays, along with the food. The baskets had to be constantly shaken or the glowing wood fragments would catch the trays on fire. If you knew what you were doing, you could easily roast the seeds without damaging the container.

Many of the Ohlones' foods were only available during certain seasons. The people moved their homes to temporary camps in order to take advantage of the abundance of food in a certain area. Some things could be preserved for later use. The fish and meat that were brought to the village by the men could be salted and smoked. The plant foods that were brought to the settlement by the women could be dried in the sun. Because of the various methods of preserving foods, the Ohlones were usually able to prepare similar kinds of meals year-round.

Arts and Crafts

The Ohlones produced remarkable artwork and crafts. They created hundreds of types of objects of exceptional strength, effectiveness, and beauty.

Nearly all Native Americans depended on stone as one of their most important resources. The Ohlones ground harder types of rocks into many different forms. Pestles, which were long stone cylinders, were used with rocks with large, round holes that were called mortars.

The Ohlones also made manos, which were fist-sized pieces of stone that looked like bars of soap. The manos were employed with slablike pieces of rock called metates. All these devices were used to crack and grind nuts and seeds. Other stone items that were made by grinding included arrow-shaft straighteners, anchors, net sinkers, and smoking pipes. As have other groups, the Ohlone produced many types of stone objects by chipping stone. These included arrowheads, drills, knives, scrapers, spear points, and many other cutting tools.

The Ohlones made many items from the animals that they hunted. Hides were used to make skirts, blankets, robes, pouches, and quivers

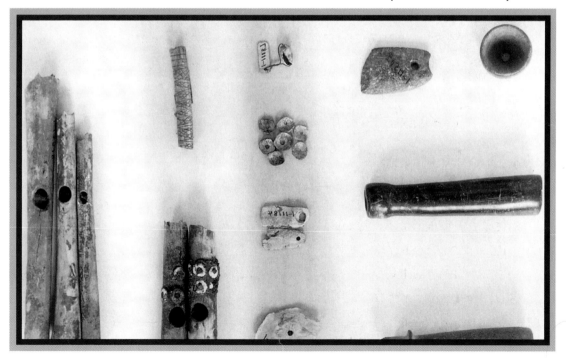

This display includes examples of Ohlone bone, shell, and ground stone objects, as well as musical instruments, shell jewelry, and a smoking pipe.

to hold arrows. Bones were made into beads, earrings, fishhooks, gambling sticks, musical instruments, nose plugs, needles, saws, scrapers, sweat sticks, and many other tools. Bird feathers were used to make or decorate arrows, bows, capes, dance skirts, headdresses, and robes. Seashells were made into bowls, fishhooks, razors, and jewelry. Turtle shells and deer hoofs were transformed into rattles. The brains of some animals, such as deer, were used to tan hides. Sinew, a kind of muscle, was removed from the bodies of deer and

This mortar and pestle was used to grind hard rocks into different shapes and forms.

combined with wood to make powerful bows. Whole ducks were stuffed with reeds to be used as decoys while they hunted.

Plants provided another important source for raw materials. Grass, rushes, fern roots, tules, and willow shoots were collected and woven into baskets by Ohlone women. Many villages had their own sets of geometric designs. Baskets were sometimes decorated with feathers and beads. Dozens of different types of baskets were made, including bowls, hats, jars, seed beaters, sifters, and trays. Wood was used to make items such as arrows, balls for sports, canoe paddles, clubs, digging sticks, earrings, fish traps, harpoons, house beams, mortars, musical instruments, nose plugs, pestles, poles, prayer sticks, snares, and stirring sticks.

The Ohlones frequently navigated the coastal areas using reed canoes, called tule balsas. These boats were made out of cigar-shaped bundles of rushes that were tied together in long bundles. Each vessel was about 10 feet (3 m) long and 3 feet (1 m) wide. The boats could hold up to four people. They were used to fish, hunt, and make journeys to nearby small islands, such as those that are found in San Francisco Bay. The tule balsas' navigators carried wooden paddles and stone anchors.

One of the most interesting pieces of hunting gear used by the Ohlones was the bola. This device consisted of a strong piece of leather or a cord made from plants and two attached weights, such as pieces of bone. When released into the air, the bola twisted. It could easily knock a bird out of the sky.

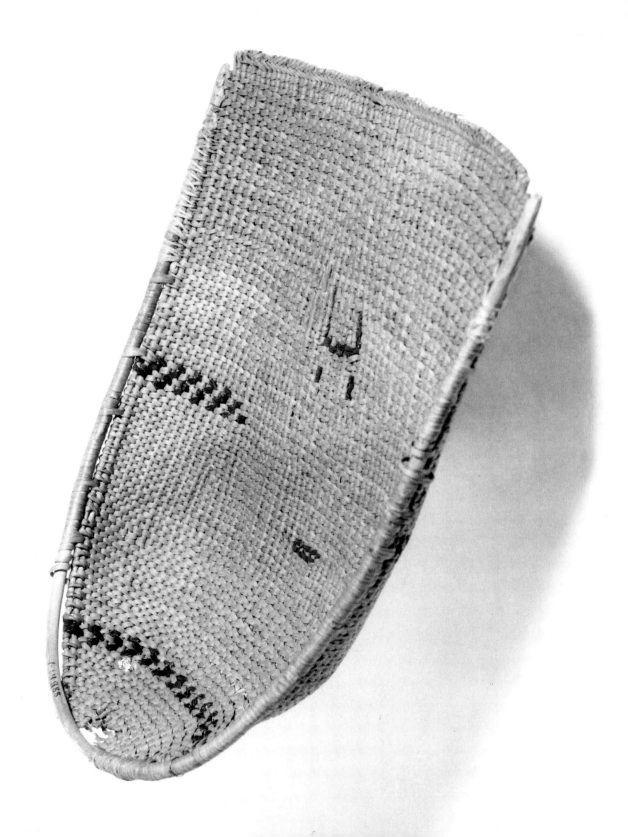

Three

Other Features of Ohlone Life

Scholars recognize that the people we call Ohlones shared certain features of social structure, government, warfare, trade, and religion. These traits make them different from their Native American neighbors. Every group of people that lives together has some kind of social structure. A community's social structure provides a way of dividing people into smaller groups. Among the Ohlones, individuals were assigned to a group based on how old they were, where they were born, whether they were men or women, and who their fathers were. To a small extent, a person's place in society was also determined by how much wealth and power they and their families had.

The smallest Ohlone social unit was the family. Most of the men had one wife. Wealthier villagers sometimes had two wives. The village chief was the only man allowed to have three wives. The work that each family member was assigned was usually determined by a person's age and gender. Ohlone families were combined into larger groups called clans. Clan members believed that their founding father was an animal, such as a deer, a condor, or an antelope. Every clan had certain religious responsibilities. The clans were further grouped into two larger units, called moieties. These were the bear moiety and the deer moiety. The moieties had specific ceremonial jobs that ensured the health and success of the Ohlone nation.

This basket was used to harvest wild grains and was made by Ohlones at Mission Soledad.

Anthropologists sometimes group all the Ohlone people who spoke the same language into social units called tribelets. Some experts feel that each tribelet was made up of several villages and formed its own nation. The people within that nation worked together and served as allies in times of war. Other researchers are convinced that the largest political group was the village.

The men who ruled the settlements were chiefs. This office was usually handed down from father to son. A council of village elders aided the chief. When the oldest son was not capable, the village council might choose someone else in the chief's family, such as an uncle, nephew, or even a daughter. The community as a whole had the right to accept or reject the new chief in a general assembly. The chiefs were given special privileges. They collected gifts of all kinds from their villagers. However, most of the items were given back to the community during religious ceremonies, or they were used to entertain guests from other communities. The scholars who believe that the tribelet was the basic political division of the Ohlones also think that each of the regions had one village that was more important than the others. The chief and council of elders of this community provided overall leadership for the tribelet.

Both men and women could become spiritual leaders. These individuals were believed to have special abilities that could be used for both good and evil. The spiritual leaders knew many special rituals, dances, and songs that were thought to have the power to make people well or sick. It was also believed that they could control the weather and the actions of some animals, such as whales. The spiritual leaders were always respected, and sometimes feared.

Government

When the Spaniards arrived to live in the region in 1770, they found between forty and fifty villages, grouped into seven language communities. Every village was surrounded by territory where its people had the right to hunt and gather. No one else was allowed to come into these areas without permission. Within their community, the people of each Ohlone village did many things that marked their differences from their neighbors. Besides speaking a different language, they often used different kinds of decorations, clothing, tattoos, and ceremonies.

Every Ohlone settlement had its village chief. These men organized the religious ceremonies, provided hospitality to visitors, and led the people during times of crisis. They also helped to arrange marriages with other villages, and sometimes led warriors on raids. The chiefs did not have the right to order people around. Most Ohlones enjoyed a great deal of freedom.

Warfare

The Ohlones conducted warfare for a variety of reasons. Sometimes the wars came about because of competition over natural resources, such as hunting and gathering areas. Other struggles developed out of accusations of witchcraft. The Ohlones fought with each other as well as adjacent Esselen, Salinan, and Yokuts peoples. Their main weapons were the bow and the spear.

Much of the fighting involved raids. Groups of young warriors would invade enemy territory and capture or kill anyone they found. The men and older women were usually slain on the spot, but the younger women and children were carried off. The victors would return to their villages with prisoners and trophies for celebrations. If they had a chance, the Ohlones sometimes destroyed whole villages. However, the wars usually ended when the chiefs of the two groups worked out a settlement.

Sometimes the Ohlone would seek to resolve their disputes with a kind of ritual battle. Both sides would meet at an agreed to place and time. The warriors wore special paint and large, feather headdresses. Speakers urged the men to bravery amid songs and dances. Eventually, one or two warriors were killed. After the deaths, one side or the other would retreat and ask for peace.

Trade

The Ohlones often traded with each other and more distant groups in order to get certain luxury items. Abalone shells, salt, various kinds of shell jewelry, and cinnabar were traded to the people living in the central valley in exchange for pine nuts. Other items that were acquired in trade by the Ohlones include black volcanic glass, called obsidian, shell beads, and special woods for making bows. The Ohlones living in the interior traded with coastal groups for salt, seashells, and other products from the sea. Strings of beads were used as a kind of money.

Religion

The Ohlones had a complex set of beliefs that provided them with a way to understand the universe and all that it contained. For example, some elders taught that the world was created during a fight between good and evil. Then there was a great flood that covered the entire world except for two islands. Everything vanished except one coyote who remained on one of the islands. A feather that floated in the surrounding waters suddenly turned into an eagle. Finally, a hummingbird joined the eagle and the coyote. Together, these three creatures made the human race. Some elders thought that this belief of creation was why the Ohlones' clans were connected to the animal world.

The Ohlones had many other religious beliefs and stories about how their world came into being. Sometimes the plots were very serious. Other stories were filled with jokes. The coyote was a particularly important figure. He was considered to be the chief of all animals. The coyote was clever, but not always reliable.

Most Ohlone holidays and celebrations were connected to their religion. Their daily life was filled with rituals that marked the

31

journey a person makes from birth to death, as well as the changing seasons. The Ohlones could tell when it was time to hold a holiday celebrating a change in the seasons by keeping track of how much time had passed since the last yearly acorn harvests. The males in the community sought various spiritual helpers that were associated with animals, such as mountain lions and coyotes. These guides would often appear in dreams.

An important idea in Ohlone worship and religious holidays was the need to balance all the power that existed in the world. If power

Deer hooves, such as the ones shown here, were sometimes strung together to create rattles that were used during dancing or worship.

shifted out of balance, sickness and death could follow. All sorts of things could contain power, including items such as animals, mountains, rivers, and even tools.

Both Ohlone men and women worshiped through songs and dance. They used musical instruments that included wooden bows, flutes, rattles, and whistles. Split pieces of wood called clapper sticks were used as drums to beat out a rhythm. The Ohlone dances often included imitations of animals. After 1770, European visitors often commented on how realistically the performers were in their presentations.

The Ohlones had dozens of religious celebrations filled with feasts, dances, songs, sporting events, and gambling. As did many Native American communities, they believed that supernatural forces and power helped to determine who would win the games. Ohlone women were particularly well known for their skills in gambling.

Many of the beliefs of the Ohlones remain unknown to the outside world. They did not create any books about their religion. Foreigners, including Spanish missionaries and soldiers, recorded the small number of descriptions of early ceremonies that have survived. Even if we knew everything that existed in the Ohlone faith, it would not be right to repeat such ideas here. Many contemporary Native Americans believe that to do so would be disrespectful, and might even harm someone. It is important that everyone's religious beliefs be treated with respect.

Four

The Ohlone and the Newcomers (1542–1900)

In 1602, Sebastian Vizcaíno became the first European explorer to make contact with the Ohlone people. This encounter took place on the shores of Monterey Bay. Vizcaíno came to California to find a location where the Spanish ships that went to the Philippines each year could stop and rest on their return voyage to Mexico. He was so impressed by the harbor at Monterey that he decided that it would be a good idea to establish a colony there. However, delays would prevent the Spanish government from building an outpost in the region for more than 150 years.

Between 1602 and 1769, other explorers and Spanish merchant ships sometimes stopped on the coast. We do not have any detailed descriptions about the things that were going on in the Ohlone territory during this time. We do know that throughout most of the New World, Europeans accidentally introduced horrible diseases that may have killed as many as 95 percent of the Native Americans. Given the frequent visits of the explorers and merchants to California, it is likely that many Ohlones suffered and died. The population had probably decreased dramatically after their first direct contacts with newcomers during the early seventeenth century. The Ohlones' numbers had probably gradually increased

Many of the Ohlones are buried in the cemetery of Mission San Francisco.

during the 150 years that followed, as they had for many other native groups living in North America.

The Ohlones and the Missions

Since the early sixteenth century, the kings and queens of Europe had claimed ownership of all of North America, although they had not actually sent soldiers to explore or occupy all of its regions. In spite of the fact that California's natives did not understand it, King Carlos III of Spain believed that he had the right to send soldiers at any time to take over anything that he wanted within their homeland. During the middle of the eighteenth century, the king became concerned about English and Russian exploration of the Pacific Ocean. He was afraid that they would send troops and ships to take over "his" territory. If California was lost, the ports of San Diego and Monterey could be used to launch invasions of Mexico and Peru, the two kingdoms that were seen as the richest parts of the Spanish Empire. In 1769, an expedition was launched to conquer California from the Native Americans. The next year, the capital of the new province was established on Monterey Bay. The outpost included a military base and a kind of religious settlement called a mission.

Spain's leaders built missions with the goal of gradually transforming the Native Americans into Spanish citizens. This goal required special men who could fearlessly work to win the Indians over without much help from the government. King Carlos III selected a group of Franciscan priests, headed by Junípero Serra, to spearhead this dangerous undertaking.

The Franciscans were anxious to go to California as missionaries. They believed that Europe had many things that could improve the lives of Native Americans, including what was then advanced technology, science and engineering. They also wanted to introduce new plants and animals to these people. In return, Ohlone knowledge about California's plants and animals could enrich the lives of the Franciscans' countrymen in Spain. The Franciscans' main goal was to build a community for God that would improve the futures of both Spaniards and the Native Americans. Between 1770 and 1835, seven missions were built for the Ohlones.

This contemporary painting from Mission San Francisco de Asís depicts the first Ohlone wedding ceremony performed at the mission.

The Making of the Missions of Sorrow

In order for the Franciscans to be able to make the missions successful, they had to persuade the Ohlones to join the new communities. Joining one of the new communities offered a number of practical benefits for the Ohlones. The Spaniards brought powerful weapons, such as ships, firearms, and steel swords. They would make good allies when the Ohlones went to war. The foreigners

This is a modern recreation of the inside of a priest's bedroom at Mission San José.

also brought steel axes, knives, dozens of new kinds of food, and animals such as horses, sheep, cattle, mules, and chickens. The Franciscan holy men also had many things of beauty, including paintings, statues, religious rituals, and powerful music.

Some Ohlones were probably attracted to the missions because of the Franciscans' preaching. Many of the priests were visionaries who offered the Native Americans a chance to build a new kind of utopia, or perfect world. Some native people may have been attracted to the Franciscans' ideals.

The missionaries reached out to the Ohlones, who decided to move to the missions as neophytes, or new followers. The village chiefs sometimes brought their whole communities to the new settlements. Once they had moved, these elders often continued to serve as leaders. The neophytes were allowed to visit and trade with non-Christian Ohlone people. They sometimes persuaded their relatives, whom the Spaniards called gentiles, to come to live with them.

Many of the Ohlones rejected the missions. Some of the people who moved into the missions decided to run away. Others tried to keep their distance from the newcomers. Many Ohlones liked the things that the Europeans brought, but did not like the foreigners' religion or the rules in the missions. Some of these people decided to work for the settlers at the military bases and towns that were founded at Monterey in 1770, San Francisco in 1776, San José in 1777, and Branciforte in 1796.

The Ohlones who lived away from the missions often felt threatened by the new communities. Although they did not understand it at the time, by building the missions, the Spaniards had given military help to some groups of Native Americans, but not others. The gentiles of rival Native American nations still saw the neophytes as their traditional enemies. To them, the creation of the missions was the same thing as a declaration of war. When they could, they raided the Franciscan outposts. The neophytes and the Spanish soldiers fought back and conducted their own raids into the gentile areas. The Europeans saw all these troubles as a kind of revolt, but to the neophytes and gentiles it represented a continuation of their traditional warfare.

The entire history of Franciscan-Ohlone contact was filled with confusion. Compared to many other coastal groups in California, the Ohlone mission communities were plagued by unrest, mass desertions, unhappiness, misunderstandings, and violence. In contrast with some of the other California Native Americans, such as the Chumash and the Luiseños, the Franciscan outposts of the Ohlone country were missions of sorrows that never achieved anything that approached the Franciscans' noble objectives.

Part of the problem was that the Ohlone Nation was filled with many small groups who spoke different languages and had different customs. The missionaries were expected to learn up to twenty languages just to be able to communicate with the people who lived in their settlement. Everything that the Franciscans tried to do was complicated by their inability to communicate or understand the diversity of the neophytes' customs and languages.

By the end of 1800, it was almost impossible for the Ohlone people to live as they once had. The gentiles could not ignore the Spaniards and their new mission societies. The foreigners and the neophytes' horses, sheep, and cattle multiplied. The animals ate traditional crops and disrupted nearly all aspects of the natural environment. Diseases killed both the neophytes and the gentiles. Some of the Native Americans who had fought the new way of life gave up and moved into the missions. Many others traveled to the north and east to join groups of Native Americans that still laid outside of the

Many Ohlones who resisted the Spanish army were captured and forced to work at the military base in San Francisco, as shown here in a depiction based on a painting by Louis Choris made in 1816.

area of European political control. A few Ohlones managed to live secret lives in the remote places near the missions in the mountains.

There were other changes caused by newcomers. Native Americans from far outside the Ohlone region, such as Yokuts, Miwoks, and Patwins, began to move into the missions. Other people from the same groups raided the remaining Ohlone gentile villages and the Spanish outposts. The Franciscans hoped that everyone would live in peace. However, serious divisions soon appeared between the Ohlones and the new neophytes. For example, the older neophytes often discriminated against the new

This replica of a Mission-period spinning wheel was made in 1939 for Mission La Purísima.

neophytes. They sometimes forced them to do the hardest work, and tried to prevent them from gaining control of important leadership positions.

By 1810, the old native world had nearly vanished. Most of the remaining Ohlone people now identified themselves with their individual missions, rather than their original nations. Some of these people showed signs of having adopted the Spanish way of life. In the more successful missions, the Ohlones helped to erect magnificent buildings and learned many European trades. The hard work of the Ohlones and other neophytes made the accomplishments of the missions possible.

Despite the conflicts that appeared between 1790 and 1821, most of the surviving Ohlone neophytes remained loyal Spanish partners. They fought hard in the struggle with the peoples living to their east and north. As members of more distant Native American groups became part of the missions, the Ohlones began to emerge as a group with a special place in mission society. Because they had lived for so long with the Spaniards, they usually knew the most about doing things in a European way. As a result, they often occupied most of the positions of leadership. Their children received all the best jobs, and they often enjoyed the best housing and other luxuries. The mission Ohlones often made fun of the new native peoples whose customs were so unlike their own, or the Spaniards'. They saw their future, for better or for worse, with the Europeans, not the gentile Native Americans.

An Uprising and an Unclear Future

By 1821, the Franciscans ran the missions with the help of Ohlone and other Native American leaders who had taken on the roles of mayor and city councilmen. From the outside, it seemed that the older neophytes who lived in the more successful missions had learned to live and think as Europeans. However, even the most willing neophytes had not completely forgotten their traditional customs. Many Ohlones mastered the new ways, but preserved what they considered to be the best of their traditions, including their language and religious stories.

In 1822, the shocking news arrived that Spain had abandoned its claim to California. Far to the south, in Mexico, rebels had won their war for independence. California, and the Ohlones, were now part of the new nation of Mexico.

Some Mexican political leaders promised the neophytes that they would soon be given complete control of the mission towns and other property. However, they worried that the Ohlone leaders would take their place in the new society of Mexico. Their promises of freedom and civil rights were never fulfilled. Delay followed delay as the Franciscans, the army, and the government in Mexico City argued about the wisdom of ending the Franciscans' role in governing the missions. In 1824, the Ohlones learned about the Chumash peoples' failed attempt to gain their rights through rebellion. After the failure of this uprising in the south, it became increasingly clear that real

There were other sources of trouble at different missions. There were Indian raids and Spanish counterattacks, particularly in the region around San Francisco Bay. There were disputes between the Franciscans and the members of the Spanish army, with civilians, and even between missionaries. Natural disasters, including epidemics, earthquakes, and floods, also took a toll. Some of the missions proved to be unhealthful. For example, Mission San Francisco was built at a place that turned out to be cold and damp. The Indians that lived there suffered horribly from many illnesses, such as arthritis, that were made worse by these conditions. Other missions were poorly located for ranches or farms. Santa Cruz, Soledad, and San Francisco made little progress. Carmel was a modest success. However, only Santa Clara, San José, and San Juan Bautista showed signs of any real progress toward the goal of transforming the Ohlones into the kinds of communities that had originally been envisioned.

freedom for the Native Americans would not be found within the European world. The priests warned the neophyte leaders that the Mexican military families were already making plans to seize the missions' lands and livestock. Soon, it would be too late.

One of the native mayors of Mission San José came up with a daring plan. Estanislao had originally been recruited from the Yokuts people in the Sierra Nevada foothills, far to the east of the Ohlones. He had quickly earned recognition as a loyal and trusted neophyte official. He had become a friend of Father Narcisa Durán, one of the most important missionary leaders. In 1828, Estanislao

Traditional native dances continued to be performed in the missions, as shown here in a depiction of a celebration at Mission San Francisco in 1816, in a painting by Louis Choris.

decided that it might be possible to build a new kind of Native American community in the far-off Sierra Nevada mountains, where he and his followers could carve out their own state.

During one of his unsupervised visits to the central valley, Estanislao led a group of followers into the foothills of the Sierra Nevada where he had been born. The other native peoples, mostly Ohlones, who were on the expedition, returned to their homes at the mission.

Estanislao rejected Christianity, but not the technology of the Europeans. He established his headquarters in a thick forest. Estanislao and his men constructed a stout log stockade and a network of tunnels. From his fortified base, he sent spies to the Ohlone missions, to invite the other neophytes to come and join them.

From his base in the Sierra foothills, Estanislao sent mounted raiders to attack various other Native American nations in the central valley. He forced several villages of these gentiles to work for him as servants and laborers. He defeated two Spanish expeditions that were sent to capture or kill him. At one point, he sent a message to the missionaries, telling them that he would soon lead an expedition to the coast and personally liberate the native people living under Mexican rule. In desperation, the government sent a third expedition against Estanislao. Mariano Vallejo headed this operation. He recruited gentiles who also opposed the former neophyte mayor. The expedition also included artillery and Ohlone warriors from Mission San José. In a bloody battle, Vallejo finally overcame Estanislao's fortress and crushed the uprising.

The defeated Estanislao fled to Mission San José, where the Franciscan in charge, Father Durán, accepted him with open arms. The missionary quickly gained a pardon for the former neophyte and attempted to have Vallejo tried for the brutality of his men, who had killed many innocent people during the recent fighting. For the remainder of his life, Estanislao remained loyal to the Mexican government and fought other Native Americans who attacked the newcomers.

The revolt was over, but time was running out for the missions. Their populations declined as Mexican officials moved to eliminate the Franciscans from government. When the end finally came, the government was supposed to give the Native American leaders, including those of the Ohlones, the control of their lands and other property. Instead, just as Father Durán had warned, a few ambitious Mexican settlers took almost everything that the Native Americans possessed.

The Ohlones After the Mission Experience

After 1835, the Ohlones faced a world of limited choices. Some became cowboys or servants. Others were captured and forced to live as slaves. Some of the Ohlones and other mission residents tried to go back to their old ways. Communities made up of mission inhabitants representing many different Native American nations grew up at places such as Alisal, near Pleasanton, and at San Juan Bautista. Other former mission neophytes joined the non-Christian Ohlones who lived around the towns at San José, Branciforte, and Monterey.

Some of the former neophytes escaped to the east and joined with other Native American peoples. They helped to organize raiding parties that captured thousands of head of cattle and horses from the Mexican ranches. By 1845, it looked as if the Native Americans might drive the newcomers out of California.

Everything changed dramatically in 1846. The Mexican-American War broke out, ending in a treaty that made California a part of the United States in 1848. The Ohlones quickly learned that the new government was no friendlier than the previous ones. The U.S. army, with its large numbers of troops and weapons, quickly crushed any Native American resistance. The politicians

This photo shows the reconstructed church of Mission Santa Clara de Asís.

from the United States believed that all of California's native peoples should be eliminated or sent away.

The Gold Rush of 1849 brought people from all over the globe to California. Within a few years, tens of thousands of these newcomers moved into the area between San Francisco and the crest of the Sierra Nevada mountains. The remaining open lands that had once belonged to Native Americans were quickly occupied without any regard to their previous ownership.

The Ohlones could do little to protect their rights from this new invasion. Although the Republic of Mexico had not treated them with fairness, the Ohlones had been made citizens with the same basic civil rights as everyone else. The United States denied nearly all Native Americans their basic rights as human beings. In 1850, the governor

Barbara Salorsano, a member of the mission community of San Juan Bautista, at age sixty in 1902.

of the new California ordered a war of extermination against the remaining native peoples. Laws were issued that made it possible for government officials to imprison poor Native Americans and make them work for free.

Despite all of the discrimination and hatred that they experienced, a few Ohlone communities, such as Alisal, survived to the end of the century. They might have continued their existence, but the U.S. government never set aside any land for them. By the end of the century, most of the remaining Ohlone people had realized that as long as they said that they were Indians, they would be stripped of nearly all their rights. Most of the survivors told the American government officials that they were Mexicans. Although these people were not treated fairly by the state or the federal government, they were not treated as badly as Native Americans. The Ohlone survivors were accepted by many poor people who were Mexicans because many of them also had Native American ancestors.

Five

The Ohlone Today

The tiny communities of traditional Ohlone people barely survived into the twentieth century. During the last one hundred years, they have struggled to protect their civil rights and rebuild their culture. Attitudes about Native Americans have changed very slowly. By 1900, many non-Indians realized how badly the Ohlones had been treated. Native Americans and newcomers worked together to improve the native peoples' lives. Gradually, some of the Ohlone families began to speak openly about their roots. In 1924, all Native Americans were finally granted citizenship. The struggle to preserve Ohlone culture and dignity has not been easily won. In 1935, only a handful of these Native Americans still spoke their language.

Despite all the horrors that they have faced, many of the Ohlones have preserved their identity as Native Americans. Today, Ohlone culture continues to grow and change. No one knows how many Ohlones are alive. Based on the evidence that is available, they probably number in the thousands. In 1971, a group calling themselves the Ohlone Indian Tribe took possession of the cemetery at Mission San José. Since then a number of other Ohlone groups, including the Amah-Mutsun San Juan Band

The Carquinez Straits near San Francisco had once been an important place in the Ohlone world. It was put to new uses by the invaders.

from Mission San Juan Bautista, and the Ohlone/Costanoan Esselen Nation of Monterey County, have been organized. The federal and the state governments have never fully acknowledged any of these groups, although they have recognized their existence in the past. As a result, the Ohlone people have never received the benefits or other support that other Native American nations have been given.

Surprisingly little evidence can be seen of the Ohlone presence in the region that was once their homeland. The modern towns and cities that surround San Francisco Bay and Monterey Bay have done little to acknowledge the contributions of the Ohlone people. A few Native American place names, such as Carquinez Straits, have survived. A small number of pieces of Ohlone artwork are preserved in Washington at the Smithsonian Institute and in a number of local museums.

The Ohlones continue to struggle against the newcomers to preserve their culture and sacred places. Some groups are trying to get the state and federal government to fully recognize them as American Indians. Other Ohlones are seeking the return of their lands. Many are angry about the removal of their ancestor's bones and other sacred things from their graves by universities and museums.

The Ohlones created an amazing way of life that lasted for more than a thousand years. They skillfully managed resources to produce a world of plentiful food. The Ohlones found their own way of looking at the world. They continue to present an important part of our nation's heritage. Everyone needs to recognize and respect their contributions and their future role in the larger American community.

Timeline

13,000–40,000 years ago	The ancestors of the Ohlones arrive in North America from Asia.
10,000 years ago	By this time, people move into the coastal area of what will one day be the Ohlone area.
500	Many of the particular patterns of life that are associated with the early Ohlones can be seen in the San Francisco and Monterey Bay areas.
1602	Sebastian Vizcaíno visits the Ohlone area and claims it for Spain.
1769	The first Spanish colonists invade California.
1770	The first military base and mission is established at the southern end of the Ohlone territory at Monterey.
1776	A second military base and mission is established at the northern end of the Ohlone territory at San Francisco.

1777	The third Ohlone mission is founded at Santa Clara.
1791	Missions are founded at Santa Cruz and Soledad.
1797	Missions are founded at San José and San Juan Bautista.
1821	Mexico becomes independent of Spain. The Ohlone people become citizens of the new nation.
1826– 1829	The Estanislao uprising fails.
1833– 1835	The missions are eliminated by the order of the Mexican government.
1846	The United States conquers California. Native Americans lose their status as citizens.
1850– 1900	Numerous laws are passed that deny Native Americans their basic human rights.
1924	All Native Americans are made U.S. citizens.
1960– present	Many Ohlones become involved in the Native American civil rights movement.

Glossary and Pronunciation Guide

anthropologist (an-thruh-PAH-luh-jihst) A scholar who studies all aspects of what it means to be human.

aqueduct (A-kwuh-duhkt) A manmade channel used to carry water.

bola (BOH-lah) A hunting device made of a piece of rope or leather with a weight tied to each end. When thrown, the bola will twist in the air and can knock down birds.

Costanoans (KOHST-ah-noh-anz) A name that was applied in the past to the peoples we now call Ohlones.

chief (CHEEF) A village leader who organized religious ceremonies, provided hospitality to visitors, and led people in times of crisis.

clan (KLAN) A group of families that claim to be related to the same animal ancestor.

clapper sticks (KLAP-per STIKS) A kind of musical instrument that was used to beat out a rhythm.

culture (KUHL-chur) Shared, learned behavior.

gentile (JEN-tyl) A word used for non-Christian Native Americans under Spanish rule.

hematite (HEH-muh-tyt) A mineral that can be used to make red paint.

manos (MAH-nohs) Fist-sized pieces of stone used with a metate to grind seeds.

metates (MEH-tot-tays) Stone slabs with bowl-like depressions, used with manos to grind seeds.

mission (MIH-shun) In colonial California, a kind of Spanish settlement where Native Americans were to be transformed into Christian citizens.

moiety (MOY-eh-tee) A kind of social unit that divides a community into two groups, based on family relationships.

neophytes (NEE-oh-fites) A term used for mission Indians who were new followers of the Christian religion.

sinew (SIN-yoo) A kind of muscle that was used in making bows.

social structure (SOH-shul STRUHK-chur) A way of dividing a community into different groups of people.

tribelet (TRYB-let) A term sometimes used by anthropologists for what the Ohlones considered to be their nations.

tule balsa (TOO-lee BAHL-suh) A kind of canoe made from bundles of reeds.

utopia (you-TOH-pee-uh) A kind of ideal community where everyone is treated fairly and is happy.

Resources

BOOKS

Campbell, Paul. *Survival Skills of Native California.* Salt Lake City, UT: Gibbs Smith, 1999.

Malinowski, Sharon (editor). *Gale Encyclopedia of Native American Tribes (Volume Three).* Detroit, MI: Gale Group, 1998.

Margolin, Malcolm. *The Ohlone Way Indian Life in the San Francisco-Monterey Bay Area.* Berkeley, CA: Heyday Books, 1981.

Milliken, Randall. *A Time of Little Choice: The Disintegration of Tribal Culture in the San Francisco Bay Area, 1769–1810.* Menlo Park, CA: Ballena Press, 1995.

MISSIONS

Mission Nuestra Señora de la Soledad
36641 Fort Romie Road
Soledad, CA 93960
(408) 678-2586

Mission San Carlos Borromeo de Carmelo
3080 Rio Road

Carmel, CA 93923
(831) 624-3600
Web site: http://www.carmelmission.org

Mission San Francisco de Asís (Mission Dolores)
3321 Sixteenth Street
San Francisco, CA 94114
(415) 621-8203
Web site: http://www.graphicmode.com/missiondolores

Mission San José
43300 Mission Boulevard
Fremont, CA 94539
(510) 657-2979

Mission San Juan Bautista
Second and Mariposa Streets
San Juan Bautista, CA 95045
(831) 623-2127
Web site: http://www.oldmission-sjb.org

Mission Santa Clara de Asís
Santa Clara University
500 El Camino Real
Santa Clara, CA 95053
(408) 554-4023

MUSEUMS

San Mateo County Historical Association and Museum
College of San Mateo
1700 West Hillsdale Boulevard
San Mateo, CA 94402
(415) 574-6441
Web site: http://www.sanmateocountyhistory.com

Santa Cruz City Museum of Natural History
1305 East Cliff Drive
Santa Cruz, CA 95062
(408) 429-3773
Web site: http://www.santacruzmuseums.org

WEB SITES

Due to the changing nature of Internet links, PowerKids Press has developed an online list of Web sites related to the subject of this book. This site is updated regularly. Please use this link to access the site:

www.powerkidslinks.com/lna/ohlone

Index